21st Century
Junior Library

TALKING ABOUT DEATH

Topics to Talk About

**AnneMarie McClain
and Lacey Hilliard**

T0001970

Published in the United States of America by Cherry Lake Publishing Group
Ann Arbor, Michigan
www.cherrylakepublishing.com

Reading Adviser: Beth Walker Gambro, MS, Ed., Reading Consultant, Yorkville, IL
Book Designer: Jen Wahi

Photo Credits: Cover: © PeopleImages.com – Yuri A/Shutterstock; page 5: © Stephanie Frey/Shutterstock; page 6: © Soloviova Liudmyla/Shutterstock; page 7: © ViaLivestream/Shutterstock; page 8–9: © Bella Barstow/Shutterstock; page 10–11: © ranaraya/Shutterstock; page 12 (left): © ta_samaya/Shutterstock; page 12 (right): © Prostock-studio/Shutterstock; page 13: © George Rudy/Shutterstock; page 14: © Prostock-studio/Shutterstock; page 15 (top): © Michal Ninger; page 15 (bottom left): © Monkey Business Images/Shutterstock; page 15 (bottom right): © koonsiri boonnak/Shutterstock; page 16: © Forewer/Shutterstock; page 18: © fizkes/Shutterstock; page 19: © Daisy Daisy/Shutterstock; page 20 (left): © Julio Rivalta/Shutterstock; page 20 (right): © Ekaterina Byuksel/Shutterstock; page 21: © Back one line/Shutterstock

Copyright © 2023 by Cherry Lake Publishing Group
All rights reserved. No part of this book may be reproduced or utilized in any form or by any means without written permission from the publisher.

Library of Congress Cataloging-in-Publication Data

Names: Hilliard, Lacey, author. | McClain, AnneMarie, co-author.
Title: Talking about death / written by Lacey Hilliard and AnneMarie
    McClain.
Description: Ann Arbor, Michigan : Cherry Lake Publishing, [2023] | Series:
    Topics to talk about | Includes bibliographical references and index. |
    Audience: Grades 2-3 | Summary: "How do we talk about death? This book
    breaks down the topic of death for young readers. Filled with engaging
    photos and captions, this series opens up opportunities for deeper
    thought and informed conversation. Guided exploration of topics in 21st
    Century Junior Library's signature style help readers to Look, Think,
    Ask Questions, Make Guesses, and Create as they go!"– Provided by
    publisher.
Identifiers: LCCN 2022039305 | ISBN 9781668920312 (paperback ; alk. paper)
    | ISBN 9781668919293 (hardcover ; alk. paper) | ISBN 9781668922972 (pdf)
    | ISBN 9781668921647 (ebook)
Subjects: LCSH: Death–Juvenile literature.
Classification: LCC BF723.D3 H556 2023 | DDC 155.9/37–dc23/eng/20220921
LC record available at https://lccn.loc.gov/2022039305

Cherry Lake Publishing would like to acknowledge the work of the Partnership for 21st Century Learning, a network of Battelle for Kids. Please visit *http://www.battelleforkids.org/networks/p21* for more information.

Printed in the United States of America
Corporate Graphics

CHERRY LAKE PRESS

CONTENTS

Let's Talk About Death   4

Dealing with Death   8

What's Most Important
to Remember?   21

Reflecting About Death   21

Glossary   22
Learn More   23
Index   24
About the Authors   24

LET'S TALK ABOUT DEATH

Death is when a **living thing** dies.

When something dies, it is not alive anymore. It cannot move or grow anymore. It cannot talk or make sounds.

After someone dies, people who cared about them may do different things. They may get together and talk about memories. They may **bury** the person or animal in a **grave** in the ground. Sometimes people and animals are turned into

4

U.S. flags are part of funerals of veterans who have died. These flags sometimes drape over the coffin. Sometimes the family will keep the flag.

ashes after they die. Their family or friends may keep the ashes in a special place or spread them out.

People use different words for death. People might say a person or animal has passed away. They might say they have lost someone, or someone did not survive. These all mean the same thing.

A living thing has died.

When an animal passes away, we can have strong feelings. Those feelings are okay!

Look!

This is a picture of a funeral. This is where someone who has died is buried in a box in the ground. How do you think the people at the funeral might feel?

There are many reasons why someone could die. Getting old is one reason. Getting very sick or having a serious accident are others. Sometimes people get a warning that a living thing will die soon. Sometimes people get no warning at all. Death can bring big feelings whether you have a warning or not.

All living things die at some point because nothing can live forever. Kids are supposed to live for a long

Ask Questions!

Find a grown-up to talk to about death. Have they ever had someone die who meant a lot to them? How did they feel?

time, though. Some people live to be 100 years or older!

There are many beliefs about what happens after a living thing dies. Some people believe when someone dies, they go somewhere special. Some believe they go in the sky and watch over people. Some believe life simply stops. Some believe you come back later as another living thing. Some believe other things.

DEALING WITH DEATH

Death is a normal part of life, but it can still be hard. When people, animals, and plants die, it can be really sad. People can also have mixed feelings.

One feeling that can come is anger. You might wish nothing ever had to die.

Another feeling that can come when something dies is confusion. You might not understand how or why this had to happen.

Make a Guess!

Imagine your friend had someone they love die. How could they be feeling? What could you try to help them feel better?

Sometimes these feelings can be really big. They may stay around for a long time or for a short time. It's okay however these big feelings show up.

Some families feel relief when someone has died because the person or animal is no longer hurting. They might feel hope because of what they believe happens after death.

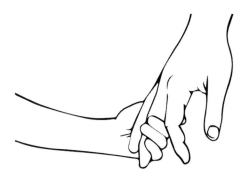

When something or someone dies, it is natural to feel all kinds of different emotions.

Kids can try things to feel more okay after a death. Talking about feelings is important. It might help to find things that remind you of who died. You can think about what they meant to you.

If someone you love has not died, you may feel glad and relieved. Some kids feel scared or worried, wondering when someone might die.

Don't let your worries get too big. It's important for your mental health to stay in the present.

There are often people left behind to grieve when someone or something dies. It is important for these people to care for their mental health.

Some children are very young when they lose a loved one. It's important for them to have someone to talk to.

WHAT'S MOST IMPORTANT TO REMEMBER?

All kids and grown-ups sometimes have to deal with death. Some kids are very young when someone they love dies.

Think!

When you think about death, do you have questions? How does this topic make you feel? Who could you talk to about it?

Some kids have more people and animals die than other kids do. It's not really fair how that works. Death is a normal part of life. It happens to everyone.

If someone you love dies, it's okay to have big feelings. There is no one right way to feel about death.

We don't have control over death, but we can support each other when it happens. It's important to be there for each other!

There's not one right way to feel about death. You could be angry, sad, worried, relieved, hopeful, or something else.

REFLECTING ABOUT DEATH

What could a grown-up do to help a kid who had someone they love die?

If you had a friend who lost a loved one, what do you think could make them feel more okay?

What do you think people should know about helping someone who has had a loved one die?

Create!

Imagine one of your neighbors had a friend who died. Make a list of things you could do to be there for them and show them love.

GLOSSARY

ashes (ASH-uhz) remains of a body after it has been cremated

beliefs (buh-LEEFS) things that are accepted or considered to be true

bury (BEHR-ee) to place a dead person or animal in the ground

confusion (kuhn-FYOO-zhuhn) state of not being able to understand something

grave (GRAYV) place where a body is buried

hope (HOHP) the wish that something will be true or will happen

mental health (MEHN-tuhl HELTH) being healthy and strong in your thoughts and feelings

mixed feelings (MIKST FEE-lings) having more than one feeling at the same time

relief (rih-LEEF) removing or lessening of something that is upsetting

LEARN MORE

Book: *Lifetimes: The Beautiful Way to Explain Death to Children* by Brian Melloni and Robert Ingpen http://www.randomhousebooks.com/books/113067

Book: *What Happens When a Loved One Dies? Our First Talk About Death* by Dr. Jillian Roberts https://www.orcabook.com/What-Happens-When-a-Loved-One-Dies

INDEX

afterlife, 9, 12
aging, 7–9
anger, 10
animals, 4–6, 12
ashes, 4–6

burial, 4, 7

confusion, 10
cremation, 4–6

death and dying, 4, 6, 7, 9, 12, 17–19

empathy, 11, 18, 20–21

feelings, 7, 9, 10–15
flags, 5
friendship and support, 11, 15, 16, 18, 20–21
funerals, 4–6, 7

grieving, 4, 6, 10–19, 21

life after death, 9, 12

memories, 4, 14
mental health, 14–15

relief, 12, 14

veterans, 5

ABOUT THE AUTHORS

AnneMarie K. McClain is an educator, researcher, and parent. Her work is about how kids and families can feel good about who they are. She especially loves finding ways to help kids and families feel seen in TV and books.

Lacey J. Hilliard is a college professor, researcher, and parent. Her work is in understanding how grown-ups talk to children about the world around them. She particularly likes hearing what kids have to say about things.